Meet my neighbor, the dentist

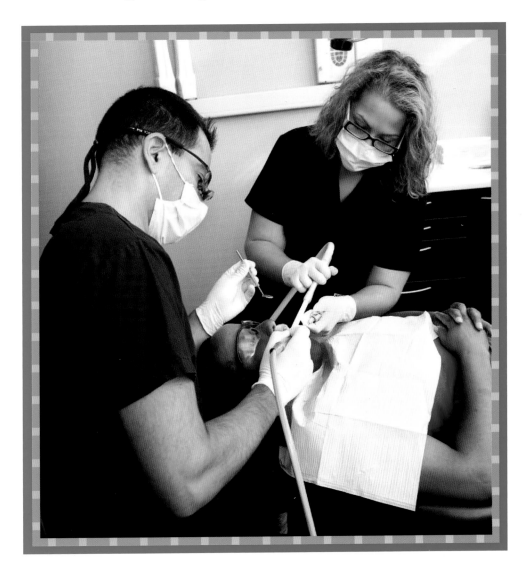

Marc Crabtree

Author and Photographer

Center for the Collaborative Classroom

Meet my neighbor, the dentist

For David and Hila, with thanks

Author and photographer
Marc Crabtree

Editor
Reagan Miller

Proofreaders
Corey Long
Crystal Sikkens

Design
Samantha Crabtree

Production coordinator
Margaret Amy Salter

Photographs
All photographs by Marc Crabtree except:
Shutterstock: pages 3, 24 (except patient and
  dental tools)

This Center for the Collaborative Classroom edition is published by arrangement with Crabtree Publishing Company.

Center for the Collaborative Classroom
1001 Marina Village Parkway, Suite 110
Alameda, CA 94501
800.666.7270 ∗ fax: 510.464.3670
collaborativeclassroom.org

ISBN 978-1-61003-355-8
Printed in China

5 6 7 8 9 10 RRD 20 19 18 17

Meet my Neighbor

Contents

Meet my neighbor, Doctor David Meisels, the dentist.

David is at home with his wife, Hila, and their daughters, Brit and Shiraz.

Brit and Shiraz help their parents make strawberry pancakes for breakfast.

At his office, David washes his hands before treating his **patient**, Jacqueline. He also puts on gloves.

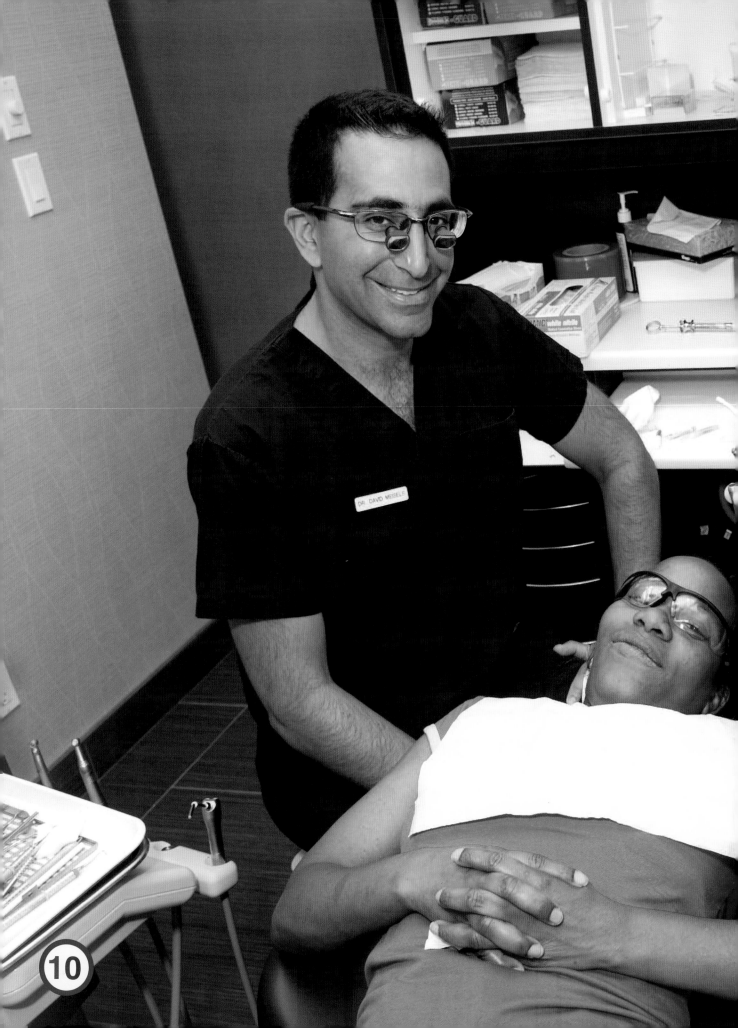

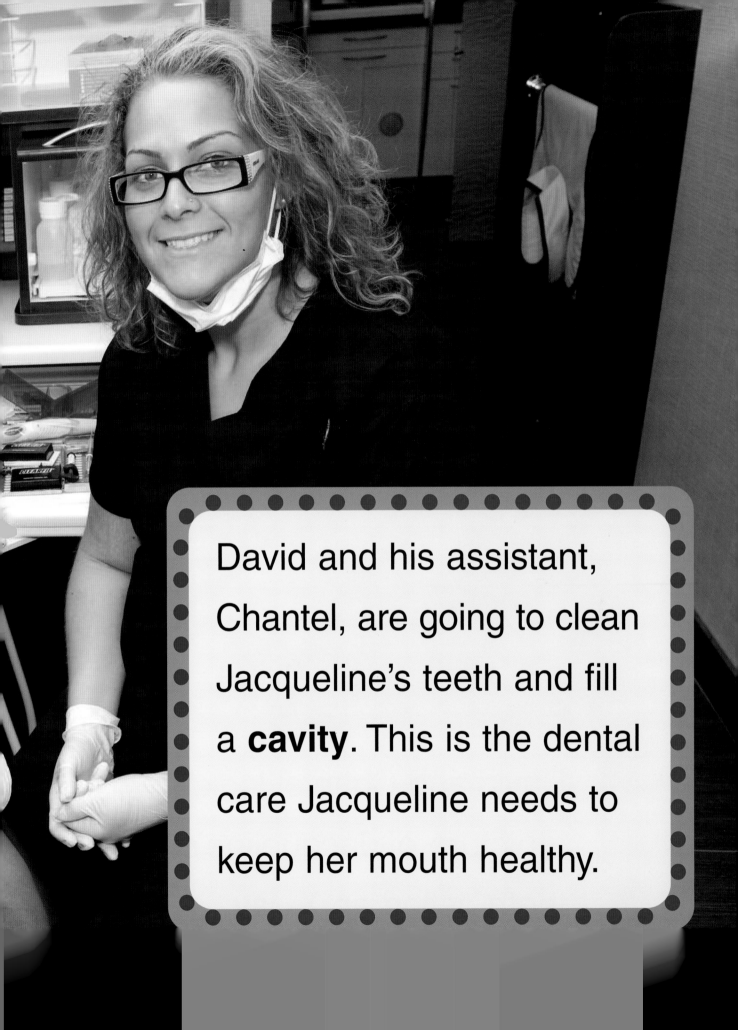

David and his assistant, Chantel, are going to clean Jacqueline's teeth and fill a **cavity**. This is the dental care Jacqueline needs to keep her mouth healthy.

David and Chantel look at a picture of Jacqueline's teeth called an **X-ray**.

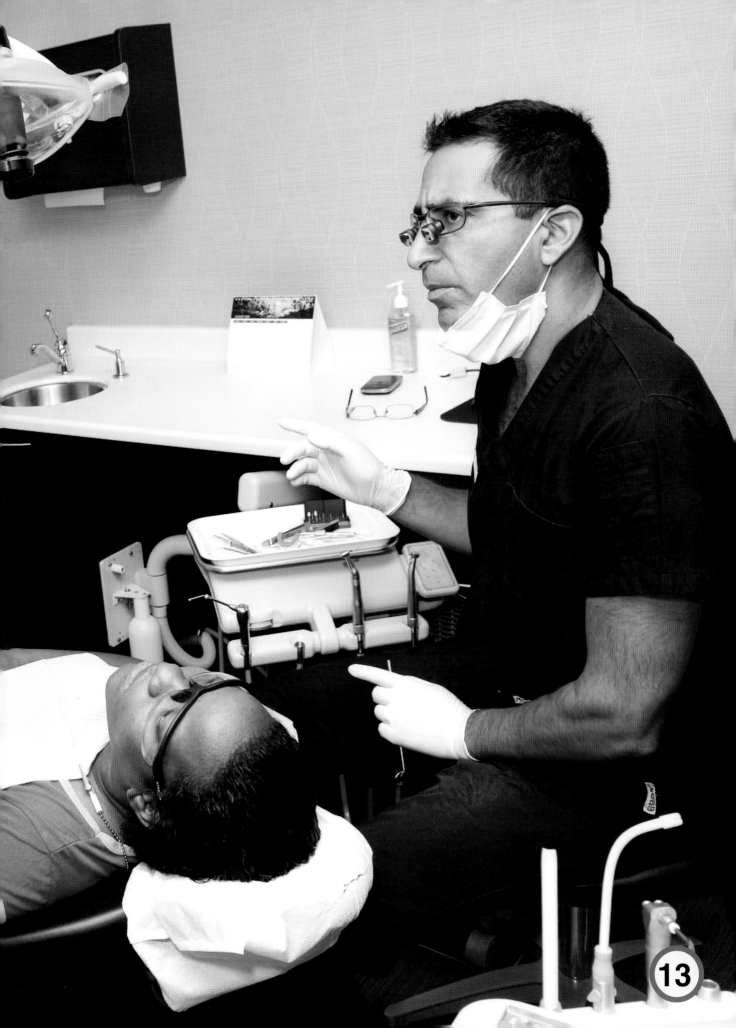

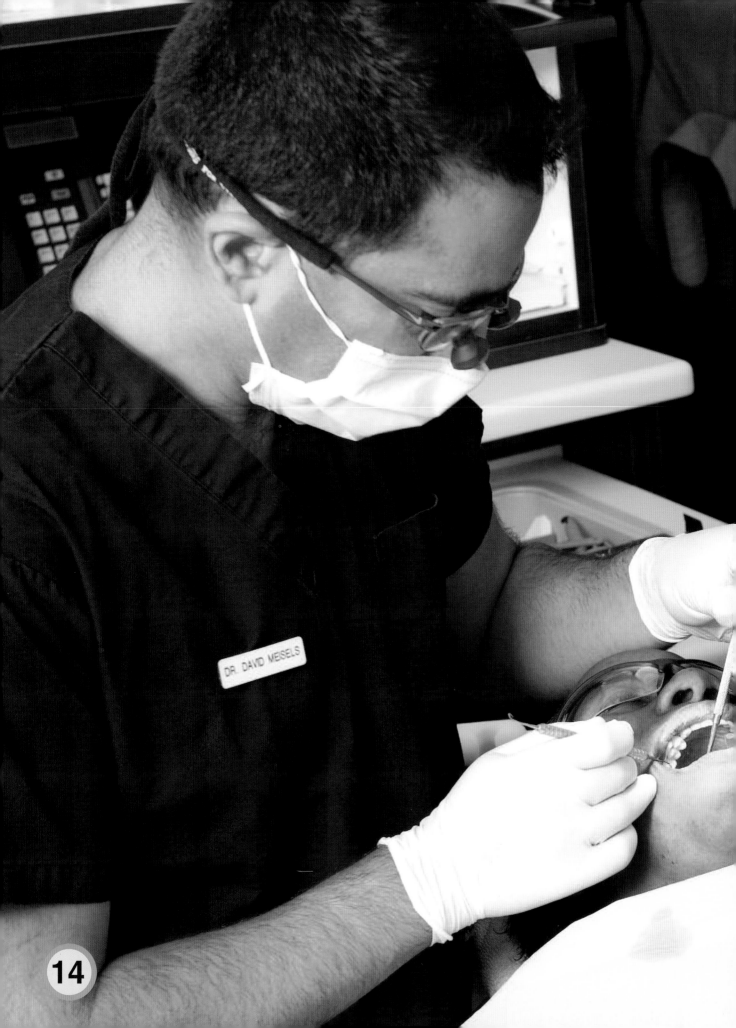

David and Chantel are cleaning Jacqueline's teeth.

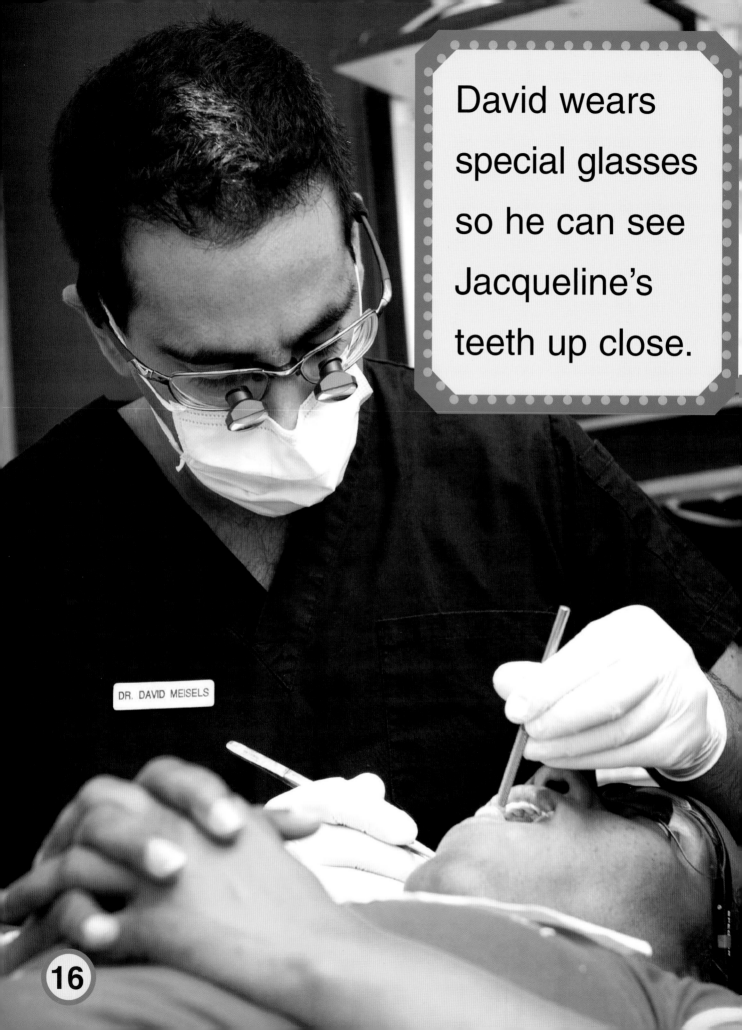

David wears special glasses so he can see Jacqueline's teeth up close.

DR. DAVID MEISELS

David is finished cleaning Jacqueline's teeth. She rinses her mouth with water.

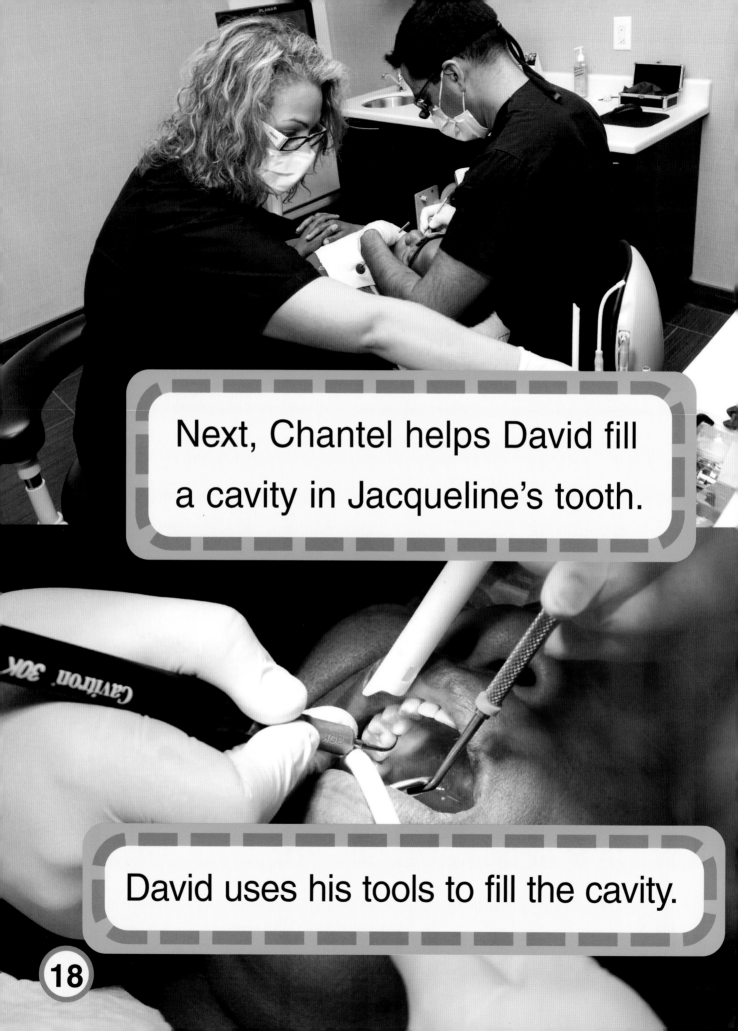

Next, Chantel helps David fill a cavity in Jacqueline's tooth.

David uses his tools to fill the cavity.

Jacqueline watches TV while David and Chantel work on her teeth.

19

Chantel shows Jacqueline how to clean her teeth using **dental floss**.

Jacqueline's appointment is done. Chantel cleans the **dental tools**.

21

Chantel puts the dental tools away in the cupboard until the next patient arrives.

Jacqueline is happy with her clean, healthy teeth. Christina, the receptionist, books Jacqueline's next appointment.

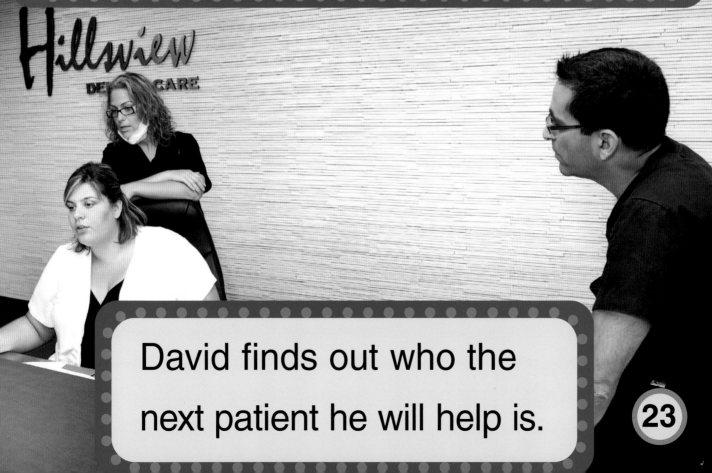

David finds out who the next patient he will help is.

Glossary

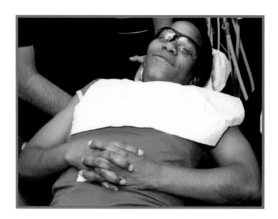

patient

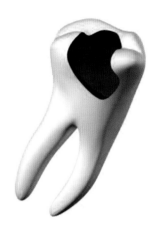

cavity

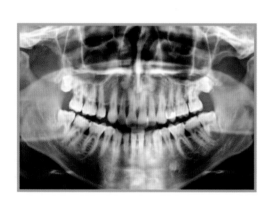

X-ray

dental floss

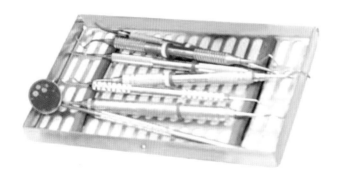

dental tools